Bankruptcy Breakthroughs

The Road to a Fresh Start

SUREN G. ADAMS

Jackson PUBLISHING

LET THE WORDS CHANGE YOU

Table of Contents

Chapter One
The Shame Myth

Introduction

The number one hurdle for most people facing financial troubles is the guilt and embarrassment associated with not paying the debts that they have amassed. The older the generation, the bigger the guilt! Ironically, for many people, major financial struggles are caused by outside forces beyond their control – job loss or income reduction, illness, or divorce – just to name a few. Why then have the guilt and embarrassment? The basis of the guilt is a misguided belief that bankruptcy is immoral because you are not paying for an obligation that you said you were going to pay. We will talk more about that in a moment. The basis of the embarrassment simply put is – pride – not wanting anyone to know that you are not "living the American dream" or not living at the financial level at which you want to be living or at the level you believe everyone else is living. Once you are able to let go of these misguided beliefs and what "people" may think of you, either because you are just too exhausted with trying to "keep it together" or simply because you have gotten to the end of your financial rope, you start to consider other options. Debt consolidation, debt settlement, debt negotiation, refinancing, loan modification, tapping into retirement savings, and then finally BANKRUPTCY! Bankruptcy is usually the last resort for many. Unfortunately, if bankruptcy were considered at the onset of financial difficulties, many sleepless nights, as well as stress, anxiety, and an unnecessary waste of money could be avoided. The worst consultations I have had as a bankruptcy attorney over the last fourteen years, are those where a client spent months and sometimes even years after a catastrophic financial event trying to fix the problem on their own while they used up all of their retirement savings trying to "catch up," with very little success. These are the worst consultations, not because I cannot help the client but because it is such a sad situation to have used up future stability for a current crisis that could have been easily avoided and resolved with the right counsel. Most retirement savings, such as IRAs, 401K, pensions, etc., are exempt in bankruptcy proceedings. Meaning that you get to keep those savings and creditors cannot go after them. Using up an exempt asset to pay down debt can sometimes be a good plan, but in a situation where there will still be debts remaining that you cannot afford, it is usually a futile and wasteful effort. I find great enjoyment and personal satisfaction in organizing and "fixing" the lives of others, so when someone uses up an exempt resource without fixing the problem it is something that is a source of great frustration for me, as well as another hard lesson for my already exhausted client.

"Is Bankruptcy Just Plain Wrong?"

I have lots of clients who come to my office not just feeling embarrassment about filing for bankruptcy, but also guilt that filing for bankruptcy is just plain wrong. My response is always the same. Bankruptcy is a Biblical principle. It is based on Deuteronomy 15: 1-11. That scripture refers to the year of canceling debt in the Jewish tradition. Every 7 years the Lord commanded the Jews to cancel the debts of any fellow Jews. They were even restricted from not giving loans in the year prior to the year of canceling debt. If we embrace the parts of the Bible about blessings and bounty, we should also embrace the parts about lack and debt. The Lord planned for the tough financial situations we may sometimes face in life. Why then ignore it and pretend it should only apply to someone else? He does not intend for people to live under the bondage of debts that they cannot afford to repay.

A good guideline to use in determining whether bankruptcy may be a good option for you is to calculate whether you would be able to repay your debt within three to five years. If not, it generally means you are making minimum payments and the debt will start to mount due to interest and penalties, rather than decrease over time. In that scenario, it is better to file for bankruptcy now and start to rebuild your credit sooner, rather than fighting a losing battle for years on end. It is the same principle as the year of canceling debt. It is better to give you a fresh start than for you to be in debt forever – that is no way to live life. Financial stress often shows up physically, in relationships, and in all sorts of other ways that are unhealthy and debilitating. There is a reason God provided this option in the Bible – He knew we would need the relief. We need to be thankful that in this country, many of our laws have a Biblical foundation, and this is one of them. Unfortunately, Congress amended the Bankruptcy Code to change the period of time between which you can file a Chapter 7 from seven years as in Deuteronomy 15 to eight years, but we still have the ability to get a fresh start and release from crippling debt if we qualify for it. So, let's look at the framework for bankruptcy to see how you qualify to file and the different types of bankruptcy relief that are available to you.

Chapter Two
The Bankruptcy Framework

Qualifying to File for Bankruptcy

Qualifying for bankruptcy depends on your income. Simply put, if you make below the median income for your household size, then you will be able to file for a Chapter 7 (having too many assets can be a problem though). If your income is above the median income for your household size, then you will need to file for a Chapter 13. The median income changes periodically and is based on the state in which you live, thus as with all things related to bankruptcy, you will need to meet with a competent attorney to determine where you are in these ranges.

A Chapter 13 also has debt limits. If your debt is above the debt limits of a Chapter 13, you will need to file for a Chapter 11. The debt limits for Chapter 13 also change periodically. There are also additional requirements for each type of bankruptcy that you must meet (of course), but these are the initial big hurdles that allow you to get into one lane or the other.

The Differences between a Chapter 7 and a Chapter 13 Bankruptcy

There are many differences between a Chapter 7 and a Chapter 13 bankruptcy, but the primary difference is usually the income of the individual that is filing the case. A Chapter 7 is reserved for people who make below a certain income level. A Chapter 13 is generally used by people who make above a certain level of income or by people who can obtain other benefits from filing a Chapter 13.

For example, as of November 2016, in Maryland, the median income for a household of one was $62,611 (*See* U.S. Department of Justice; 2017). If you make less than the median income you can file for a Chapter 7 bankruptcy. When you file for bankruptcy, you are allowed to keep a certain amount of assets, which vary from state to state. In order to file for a Chapter 7, you should also be sure that your assets would be exempt, so that when you file, you get rid of all your debt, and keep all your assets. For example, currently in Maryland, you are allowed to keep approximately $12,000 in assets and about $23,000 in equity in your primary residence when you file for bankruptcy (*See* Md. Code Ann. § 11-504). Therefore, if you are a single person and you have the following stats:

- Annual income: $55,000,
- One car that has a loan on it with no equity
- A condo with a mortgage and $20,000 in equity

- Bank account balance = $1000
- Household furniture and electronics = $5,000
- Debts you cannot afford to keep up with = any amount

With the above statistics (as of November 2016), you could file for a Chapter 7 bankruptcy and eliminate all of your dischargeable debt (*See* Md. Code Ann. § 11-504).

If your income is more than the median income, then you will need to do a Chapter 13 bankruptcy. The Chapter 13 bankruptcy is a three to five-year repayment plan. In the plan, you repay some (or all) of your debt based on your disposable income and the amount of non-exempt assets.

The median income for a household of two in Maryland as of November 2016, is $80,492 (*See* U.S. Department of Justice; 2017). If, for example, you are a married couple and you are making $100,000 jointly, you would need to file a Chapter 13 bankruptcy. However, if you make less than the median income, but you own a home that has $100,000 worth of equity, then you will also need to file for a Chapter 13 because you have too much to lose in filing a Chapter 7.

A Chapter 7 is a liquidation type of bankruptcy. If you have non-exempt assets, which are assets over the amounts that you can exempt in your state, then your Chapter 7 Trustee can liquidate those assets to pay your creditors. Obviously, you do not want to risk losing your house or other valuable assets to a Trustee sale in a bankruptcy, therefore you would not file a Chapter 7 if you have significant non-exempt assets that you would want to keep. Instead, you can file a Chapter 13 or a Chapter 11 bankruptcy, and pay the creditors through the payments of your repayment plan, the amount that the creditors would have received if you had filed a Chapter 7 liquidation case. The benefit of this option is that you can consolidate your debt payments into one repayment plan payment to the Trustee and stretch them out over a three to five-year period. Also, depending on the amount of non-exempt assets, you can potentially still get a discharge of some of your debt. You can also then limit interest from accruing on the debt while you are in the plan.

There are also times when you would *qualify* to file for a Chapter 7, but you *should* file for a Chapter 13 anyway because there is a benefit you can gain from the Chapter 13 that you cannot have in a Chapter 7. The biggest of these benefits is the ability to eliminate a second mortgage in a Chapter 13. If your home is worth less than the amount of your first mortgage, you can "strip off" the second mortgage in a Chapter 13. During the Chapter 13 plan, the second mortgage is considered an unsecured creditor, like a credit card. At the end of the plan, it gets discharged like the other unsecured debts that did not get paid in the plan. The added benefit is that the second mortgage company also has to release their lien on your house! So, after the discharge, you will have eliminated your unsecured debts and your second mortgage!

Let's look at this with an example to make it more clear. John and Jane Smith have a combined median income of $80,000. They fell behind in their mortgage when Jane was on maternity leave after a difficult pregnancy. They now have $50,000 in medical bills, $15,000 in credit card debt, $5,000 in mortgage arrears, and $2,500 in tax debt. Their house is worth $150,000, but they owe $175,000 to their first mortgage company and $50,000 to their second mortgage company. The Smiths qualify for a Chapter 7 bankruptcy, which would get rid of their medical bills and credit card debt. However, their tax debt is too recent to be discharged. Also, a Chapter 7 will discharge their mortgages, but that will not help them to get caught up and stay in the property. Although the mortgage note would be discharged, the mortgage companies could still foreclose on the deeds of trust they still hold on the property itself due to the Smith's non-payment. When you purchase a house, you sign two documents: a promissory note and a deed of trust. The note is what is discharged in bankruptcy, but the deed of trust is what is still recorded in the land records and what gives the mortgage company the right to foreclose if the promissory note is not paid. Therefore, the best option for the Smiths is to file a Chapter 13 bankruptcy. It is not only the best option; it is actually a great option for them. Here's what it will do. Due to the fact they are actually below the median income, they can do a three-year plan rather than the five-year plan but we will want a low monthly fixed plan payment, so we will pick a five-year plan. In that plan, we will pay off their tax debt because it is a priority creditor that has to be paid in the plan. That is good for them because the tax debt is non-dischargeable since it is a recent tax bill, so we want it to be paid in the plan. We will also pay their mortgage arrears in the plan because that is also a priority debt since it is a secured arrears. Which is also good because they want to keep their house. What they don't want is the second mortgage payment, which they will get to stop paying while they are in the plan. We will file a motion to strip that second mortgage off their home because the first mortgage amount is more than the house is even worth. While the Smiths are in the plan, they will pay their first mortgage, their car payment, their regular utilities and household expenses, and a plan payment of about $140 based on what debts the plan needs to pay (mortgage arrears, tax payment, and administrative fees). At the end of the five years, the Smiths will be caught up on their mortgage, they will have paid off their taxes, and they will get a Chapter 13 discharge of the medical, credit card, and second mortgage debt. AND the second mortgage company will have to record a Release of their deed of trust lien in the land records office that they originally had against the Smith's house. The Smiths will emerge from the bankruptcy with just one mortgage. By the end of their plan, their car note would also likely be paid off and they would otherwise be debt-free and can have a fresh start. This is how bankruptcy was intended to work or at least if applied to your situation by a skilled and experienced attorney.

A Chapter 11 Bankruptcy

A Chapter 11 bankruptcy is primarily reserved for businesses that want to reorganize. For example, if you have a business that you want to keep open but you have overwhelming debt, you can file a Chapter 11 and set up a payment plan that can help keep your business afloat. It is a very complex type of bankruptcy and can also be used by individuals who are over the Chapter 13 debt limit. As of 2016, your secured debt must be under $1,184,200.00 and your unsecured debt must be under $394,725.00 in order to qualify for a Chapter 13 bankruptcy (*See* 11 U.S.C. § 109(e)). Otherwise, you will need to file a Chapter 11 or if you are below the median income, a Chapter 7. There are other types of bankruptcies like a Chapter 9 for municipalities, or a Chapter 12 for family farmers or fishermen. For most individuals, they will fall under a Chapter 7 or a Chapter 13.

Let's get into some more of the specifics of how the bankruptcy process works and answer some of the common everyday questions that we hear.

Chapter Three
Common Questions Answered

How Long Does a Bankruptcy Case Take?

A Chapter 7 takes approximately three months from the filing of the case to the discharge date. A discharge means that you are no longer legally responsible for the dischargeable debt. Within approximately two weeks after the discharge is granted, if there are no outstanding issues in your case the court will issue a final decree, which will close the bankruptcy case.

A Chapter 13 case takes three to five years for the repayment plan. If you are over the median income for your household size, you automatically have to do a five-year repayment plan rather than a three-year plan.

In one particular Chapter 13 case of mine, my client had a primary residence where we stripped off a second mortgage , and a rental property where we stripped off a second mortgage. Her plan actually concluded in about a year because many of her creditors did not file claims in her case, which meant that her plan payments quickly paid off the creditors who did file claims. This is unusual but in this particular case her Chapter 13 ended in one year, she received her discharge, and the second mortgages on both of her properties were stripped off. By the time the bankruptcy was concluded, the value on her rental property had actually increased and she was able to sell it for a profit because of the fact that the second mortgage was stripped off. She not only obtained a fresh start with her debt being discharged, but she regained equity in her properties from stripping off the second mortgage liens.

How Many Court Appearances Are There When I File for Bankruptcy?

Court appearances vary based on the type of bankruptcy that you file. For example, in a Chapter 7, there is usually no court appearance, there is typically just a creditors' meeting with the trustee assigned to your case by the court. The trustee is an attorney who has been hired by the U.S. Trustee's Office to represent the interest of the creditors in your case. The U.S. Trustee is also in charge of making sure the Bankruptcy Code is being followed. The trustee assigned to your case will hold a creditors' meeting about 30 days after the case is filed. In Maryland, the location of your creditors' meeting is determined based on the county in which you currently live. For example, if you live in Prince George's County, your creditors' meeting will be held in Greenbelt in the U.S. Trustee's Office. If you live in Anne Arundel County, your creditors' meeting will be held in Baltimore in the U.S. Trustees Office at the U.S. District Courthouse. In D.C., the creditors meetings are held in one of the courtrooms in the U.S. District Court in the District of Columbia. The creditors' meetings are administrative meetings and are not conducted by a judge.

Creditors meetings tend to last anywhere from a minimum of five minutes up to about sixty minutes. I love seeing the relief on my clients' faces when their creditors meeting takes only a few minutes. This happens when schedules are well-prepared, documents are filed with the Trustees' offices and with the courts on time, and when your attorney has experience with what to do in the meeting itself. I prepare my clients for the creditors meeting even from the initial consultation, which results in meetings that are fast and stress-free. My goal is for my clients to leave the creditors' meeting with a sense of relief and feeling excited about the end of their case when they can start afresh.

In a Chapter 13 case, after the creditors' meeting is held, there is also a confirmation hearing. In most Chapter 13 cases, appearances at the confirmation hearing are waived if the trustee recommends confirmation of the plan that is submitted.

Can I File an Individual Bankruptcy If I am Married?

Yes, you can file for an individual bankruptcy if you are married. However, the court will look at your total household income and total household expenses. Therefore, you still need to report your spouse's income and expenses even if you are filing individually. Notably, the bankruptcy will not affect a non-filing spouse's credit score if they continue to pay any debts on their credit report. If you file individually, your bankruptcy would not show up on your non-filing spouse's credit report and it will not affect their individually held debt or their individually held assets. I always recommend to clients who are married that even if their spouse has their own set of debts, they should file jointly so that the joint household can move forward after the bankruptcy – debt-free together. If you are filing individually and your spouse still has debt, you are still going to be feeling the effect of that separate debt on the household budget after the bankruptcy. There are situations though, where one spouse has all of the debt in their name. In that situation, it makes more sense for just the one spouse to file, even if the other spouse's income is included in the bankruptcy calculations.

Do I Have to List All of My Debts When I File for Bankruptcy?

Yes, you have to list all of your debts and all of your assets when you file for bankruptcy. In fact, you have to sign under penalty of perjury that you have done just that. The reason for this is that the court needs a full picture of your finances in order to make a decision about whether you can obtain a discharge. Even though you list all of your debt you can reaffirm some debt, which means that you agree with the creditors to take it out of the bankruptcy discharge. The only type of debt that you would ever want to do that with is a reasonable vehicle loan, where you intend on keeping the vehicle. The main reason for doing this is so you can get the benefit of the on-time payments established on your credit report, which will then help to rebuild your score after the bankruptcy. I have lots of clients who have houses with mortgages that get included in the bankruptcy discharge, because we do not formally reaffirm the mortgage debt because that is a huge amount to be "back on the hook for" after a bankruptcy discharge. In Maryland, you have to be over three months behind on your mortgage in order for a mortgage company to foreclose on your property. Therefore, as long as you keep up-to-date with your payments, a mortgage company cannot foreclose on your property even though the mortgage is included in your bankruptcy discharge. After the full mortgage is paid off they then release their lien on your property in the form of a Deed of Trust. The benefit of getting a mortgage included in the discharge is that if you decide you no longer want to stay in that property you are no longer financially responsible for the mortgage. If that situation happens, I always recommend doing a short sale if your house is upside down, or even a regular sale, rather than just walking away from the property and having the mortgage company foreclose. A foreclosure is much more damaging on your credit report than a short sale, and you would have most likely rebuilt your credit after the bankruptcy and would definitely not want something like a foreclosure on your credit after already rebuilding from a bankruptcy.

All of your debt must be listed on your bankruptcy and if it is a dischargeable debt, it will be included in the discharge unless you reaffirm the debt. You can also choose to voluntarily pay for any debt that has been discharged, such as a debt to a family member or friend.

What Can I Keep When I File for Bankruptcy?

Each state in the U.S. has a list of items that are "exempt" from creditors, meaning that they cannot be taken even if you owe someone a debt that you haven't paid. These are basic "necessities" that you can keep and that creditors can never go after. Those exempt items are exempt in a bankruptcy filing as well. Some states allow you to use federal exemptions instead of the state exemptions and you can pick between the two. The District of Columbia is one of those "states" that allow both federal and local exemptions. Maryland, however, has its own exemptions and you cannot use the federal exemptions in Maryland. As of November 2016, in Maryland, you can keep approximately $12,000 worth of assets . There is about $1,000 for household goods, $5,000 for personal property, and $6,000 for what is called a "wildcard" exemption. Also, in Maryland we have a somewhat new homestead exemption of approximately $23,000 of equity that you can keep in your primary residence. Each individual has these exemptions that they can use. When you file for bankruptcy, you must list all of your assets and apply the appropriate exemptions so that you can keep them.

Sometimes there are hard decisions that you have to make when you are filing for bankruptcy if you have been living beyond your means for a long period of time. Bankruptcy will give you a fresh start, but you have to be willing to fully look at your situation and not allow yourself to get back into the same mess that you were in before. For example, I have had families come to me overwhelmed with the cost of living in this area. When we actually looked at their finances, hard decisions had to be made about private schools, high car notes, and their mortgages and what their salaries could actually support. In one particular case, I had a couple who surrendered their house in their bankruptcy! We also did a short sale on the property so they would not have a continuing HOA liability after the discharge. They also surrendered one of their vehicles in the bankruptcy and we were able to get them a redemption loan on their other vehicle, which is a loan that refinances the vehicle at a fair market value. They were able to get rid of all of their credit card debt under bankruptcy. Moving on, they learned to live within a budget that was more realistic for their family instead of trying to live beyond their means. They rented a home in a neighborhood where their daughter could go to an excellent public school. Recently, that same couple purchased a home that they could easily afford and are back on the road to building equity after only three short years! After you file for bankruptcy, you are required to take certain financial courses. One of the courses that you are required to take is a financial management course, and it really helped them to develop and plan out a budget that they could stick to. Sometimes filing bankruptcy can be a good opportunity to ask yourself "What do I really need?" rather than "What can I keep?"

How Does Bankruptcy Affect a Security Clearance?

Bankruptcy can negatively affect your security clearance. Most government agencies will let you know that filing for bankruptcy can have a negative impact on your security clearance but they will not be very specific in terms of what that effect is. For the most part my experience has been that agencies will use a bankruptcy filing as the reason for getting rid of you if they already had a previous reason to get rid of you. If you are in good standing with your current employer and you are up-front with them about the fact that you are filing for bankruptcy, then it usually has little to no affect. I have had hundreds of clients with security clearances but I haven't had a single-one with a clearance that has been fired from a government agency after filing for bankruptcy. Again, I always recommend that you always be up-front with your employer or your HR manager, to prevent it from being a surprise to them. Especially if you think that it could potentially be an issue. Let them know ahead of time that you have a financial situation that you are resolving by filing for bankruptcy. You are much more of a risk to your employer if you are carrying lots of debt that you can't afford to pay back than you are if you are filing a Chapter 7 bankruptcy and getting rid of the debt or filing for a Chapter 13 bankruptcy and making a plan to repay the debt.

Does Anyone Need to Know That I Filed for Bankruptcy?

Yes, and no, because bankruptcy is public record. If someone did a search on the Pacer database, which is a federal database of court cases, or even pulled your credit report, then they would be able to find the fact that you previously filed for bankruptcy. Unless you tell someone that you filed, they most likely would never know without doing that specific kind of search to find the information. For example, I have had clients who have been worried that bankruptcy would be posted in the newspaper. Unless you are a high-net-worth individual or a big business owner, personal bankruptcies don't usually make the news.

Will I Be Able to Keep My Retirement Savings If I File for Bankruptcy?

I had an elderly client who came to me with an overwhelming amount of credit card debt that she had accumulated after her husband had passed. She was using credit cards to pay for her living expenses. She then started trying to catch up on these credit cards by using her retirement accounts, which was really upsetting to hear because retirement accounts are fully exempt in a bankruptcy. She could have just simply gotten rid of that debt and kept all of her retirement assets if she had filed for bankruptcy instead of trying to handle the situation on her own. Thankfully, she came to my firm before she had spent all of her retirement assets and we were able to save the remainder of her retirement as well as get rid of all of her unsecured debts.

The question of whether you can keep retirement savings when you file for bankruptcy is an important one because assuming the incorrect answer can cost you tens of thousands of dollars in not just retirement funds, but future tax liability as well. Most retirement assets are exempt when you file for bankruptcy. I have had several clients who have struggled with paying their mounting debts and have made the mistake of pulling out their retirement savings to pay for the debt. In doing so, they then incurred a tax liability for the retirement withdrawals. That is one of the things I never want to hear from clients in our initial consultation because those retirement assets are generally fully exempt. If you end up needing to file for bankruptcy anyway after using up your retirement funds, you have essentially wasted assets in paying off debts that could have been completely dischargeable. Thankfully, if you seek competent help first, you can save those assets that are intended for your retirement years.

Should I Make Any Changes Right Before Filing for Bankruptcy?

I often get asked "Should I sell my assets right before filing or transfer them to someone else, so that my assets will be below exemptions?" The answer is always "ABSOLUTELY NOT!" Transferring assets right before a bankruptcy in order to protect those assets from creditors is a fraudulent conveyance, which can get you thrown in federal prison. It is NOT worth it! There are recent celebrity examples of this to prove it can happen. Lying about your assets or transferring them prior to bankruptcy can easily be determined by the U.S. Trustee's office, which is part of the Department of Justice, and they WILL prosecute. They can even look back over a period of the last two years for such transfers. Those types of transfers have to formally be disclosed on your bankruptcy documents; failure to disclose them is also a federal crime. Therefore, it is extremely important that if you have a question about whether you would be able to keep something or even how to do something prior to filing for bankruptcy, that you check with an experienced attorney before doing anything. Always follow your competent attorney's advice. There are often legal methods of handling certain assets that you may not be aware of and that your attorney will have more knowledge of and experience with handling within the strict guidelines of the law. There is no need to put yourself in jeopardy of committing a crime when the goal of the bankruptcy is to give you a fresh start.

Which Debts Are Dischargeable?

If the bankruptcy court grants a discharge in your Chapter 7 case, you are no longer legally obligated to pay dischargeable debts, which include the following:

- credit card balances;
- deficiencies on auto repossessions;
- medical bills;
- judgments; and
- personal loans.

In order for debts to be discharged, they must exist on the date that the bankruptcy case was filed and be properly listed in the bankruptcy. Creditors are prohibited from attempting to collect a debt that was discharged. That means that creditors cannot contact you by mail, phone, or otherwise. They cannot file, continue a lawsuit, or attach wages or any other property. However, creditors may have the right to enforce valid liens, such as mortgages or auto liens. That means that the creditor can take back the secured property if you do not keep up with payments on the debt, regardless of the discharge.

Which Debts Are Not Dischargeable?

Even if the bankruptcy court grants a discharge in your Chapter 7 case, you are still legally obligated to pay some debts such as:

- most taxes;
- debts incurred to pay non-dischargeable taxes;
- domestic support obligations;
- student loans;
- most fines, penalties, forfeitures, or criminal restitution obligations;
- debts for personal injuries or death caused by the debtor's operation of a motor vehicle, vessel, or aircraft while intoxicated;
- debts owed to certain pension, profit sharing, stock bonus, other retirement plans, or for certain types of loans from the Thrift Savings Plan for Federal employees;
- debts the bankruptcy court has specifically decided are not discharged; and
- debts that have been reaffirmed.

Chapter Four
Rebuilding Your Finances

The moments after getting a Discharge Order notice from the court are some of the most exciting two minutes of my days in practicing law. It will sound silly to most, especially if you are a fire fighter, or a medical doctor, or someone doing something "life or death" for a living. Even so, here is how it happens. The bankruptcy system is in the federal court system, which is an all-electronic system (which is great). We get all the notices on our cases electronically in our e-mail and we file everything electronically, as well. When the objection deadline of sixty days from the creditors' meeting has passed without objection, the court clerk will issue the Discharge Order in a Chapter 7 case (it's a lot more complicated in a Chapter 13, so we'll focus on a Chapter 7). That will then show up in my inbox as an e-mail from the court, which is super easy to spot, and it is equally easy to spot the words Discharge Order. The moment I see that pop up on my screen, I stop everything and immediately get so excited for my client. I e-mail them right away because it's like wanting your kids to open their presents on Christmas morning – you just can't wait to see how happy they are. Sure enough, I will get an immediate email back from an equally excited client and in that moment, I've had the best two minutes of my day!

After the bankruptcy case has concluded, the court will send the Discharge Order and Final Decree to all of your creditors and your discharged creditors will begin to show zero balances on your accounts due the bankruptcy. It is illegal for creditors to continue collection activity on discharged debts.

What to Do If Creditors Contact You

I had a client who was still receiving notices from a mortgage company whose lien was stripped in her chapter 13 case, even after her bankruptcy was discharged. The mortgage company actually released the lien but due to a technical error in their database, notices kept being sent to her about owing the mortgage. We sent them numerous notices and due to a provision under the Bankruptcy Code, I connected my client with a litigation colleague who sued the bank on her behalf. She was able to recoup penalties and fines because of the fact that they did not fix their computer error, and continued contacting her after the debt was discharged.

There are remedies in place to stop creditors from illegal collection of discharged debt after bankruptcy. If you are contacted by a creditor after your case is discharged, keep good written records of the contacts, notify the creditor of the discharge in writing, and notify your attorney.

The Impact of Bankruptcy on Your Credit

Because I live about five minutes from my office, I often bump into my clients at the grocery store or when I am "out and about" with my family. I especially love when this happens after a client's case has been discharged because they are always so happy to see me and excited to tell me how well things are going for them. I have had many clients who say they now have an "Excellent" credit rating.

A Bankruptcy will stay on your credit for up to ten years after the filing of the bankruptcy. The primary question most people will have is, "What impact will bankruptcy have on my credit?" The answer to that question can be surprising. Obviously, filing for bankruptcy will have a negative impact on your score, initially. However, many people don't realize that within about a year after the filing of a bankruptcy most of debtors report an increase in their credit score. The score for most of my clients goes up anywhere from 50 to 100 points in the year following the bankruptcy filing. That increase can be attributed to the zero balances that will be reported on your credit report due to the bankruptcy discharge. After the discharge is entered and your creditors start reporting to the credit bureaus that you have a zero-balance due to the bankruptcy discharge your score should start to increase. What keeps your score increasing is on-time payments on any debt that you keep or acquire after the bankruptcy. For example, a non-dischargeable student loan or if you keep a vehicle loan through reaffirmation in a bankruptcy, those debts will show up on your credit report post-bankruptcy. If you are making on-time payments on that debt, that will keep your score increasing. Another method for increasing your credit score after a bankruptcy is by getting a credit card -- either a secured card or a regular credit card. I know that sounds counterintuitive, but yes, getting a credit card! Being able to use a high-risk debt like a credit card post-bankruptcy is the fastest method to rebuild credit-worthiness, as well as your credit score. The key is using the credit for the purpose of increasing your score, NOT for acquiring things or even for emergency purchases. Credit cards should not be used for emergencies. You should create an emergency savings account as soon as you file for bankruptcy and start to put the amounts you were spending on your credit cards in that account immediately. When an emergency comes up, which it will, you can borrow from yourself. Then proceed to pay yourself back, without having to pay exorbitant or crippling interest. The way to use a credit card to rebuild your score is to use it to purchase nominal things, like getting gas once or twice a month. Let the bill arrive so that you are in a billing cycle and PAY THE BILL ON-TIME. That is the most important part of rebuilding your credit. It actually becomes fun to use credit "against" the credit card companies. For example, you can use a store card to get the discount being offered and pay the card off right after (with the same salesperson – the reaction is priceless). Once you become a pro at the credit game, you can proceed to use cards that offer points or miles for things you already have to pay for anyway. You can set-up automatic payments from your bank accounts to pay the card off at the intervals where you will get the points, but not be charged any interest. Responsible use of credit, paying your debt on time, never using any credit card up to its maximum or even past 25% of its limit, are the primary ways to rebuild your credit after a bankruptcy filing. The reality is, the impact to your credit score after a bankruptcy is negative for about a year and after that you can quickly see your score increasing and surpassing where it was previous to filing.

I have had clients who reported getting lots of credit card and car offers in the mail after filing for bankruptcy because the credit card companies know that you have more disposable income after a bankruptcy discharge. It is very important that you are responsible with credit after bankruptcy as you can quickly get yourself back into the same situation if you are not careful. Also, you can't file another chapter 7 for an additional eight years after previously filing a chapter 7. Some clients take this warning, go overboard, and never use credit again, which is even worse. If you don't use credit whatsoever, your credit will never improve. You must use credit responsibly in order to build good credit. With good credit, you will have more financial options in the future.

When Can You Buy a House After Filing for Bankruptcy?

The FHA guideline is two years (lenders may add additional requirements) after a Chapter 7 bankruptcy. Although, there is no wait period after a Chapter 13 or if you are doing conventional financing!

Bankruptcy is like marriage. It should not be entered into lightly. You should always hire someone with knowledge and experience who you can trust to guide you through the process or things can go extremely bad, very quickly. When done properly, bankruptcy can yield wonderful results.

Works Cited

"Census Bureau Median Family Income By Family Size." *Cases Filed On or After November 1, 2016.* The U.S. Department of Justice (DOJ), U.S. Trustee Program, 15 Jan. 2017 Web.

Md. Courts and Judicial Proceedings Code Ann. § 11-504 (2017).

11 U.S.C. § 109(e), with applicable adjustments of dollar amounts from 22 Feb. 2016 Fed. Reg. Vol. 81, No. 34.